Ethereal

Angel Selena Quintana

Cyberwit.net
HIG 45 Kaushambi Kunj, Kalindipuram
Allahabad - 211011 (U.P.) India
http://www.cyberwit.net
Tel: +(91) 9415091004 +(91) (532) 2552257
E-mail: info@cyberwit.net

Printed at Repro India Limited.

Dedication:

To all who will read my words, thank you.

A.K. you are always my North star and more, till the world explodes and what is past.

My grandparents who believe in me, I thank you for all and beyond.

Love you more mom.

Contents

Sink

I want to lay in a grass field
To feel nothing but warmth
The sun's rays radiating through my veins

Still
No bounds
Let the caress of the soft earth deteriorate my inner constrictions

I am warmth
You are my sun
We are a world lost
Let's watch its ruins together

Sight

Pixie dust fades to cigarette ashes
Sunsets over city lights

A tinge of monotony
Because there was never vivid honesty

Hold me as I shatter
And my glass persona cuts your paper soul

Vision Scenery

Light from a window pane
Reflects my eternal pain
Burning, jagged, flaring bright

Light from within singed
Flaring bright pain
Searing sight

Light, enlightening, lighting
Light embodies and reflects both ways

Shining out, Lashing out
Transparency is my discrepancy

Wash it away like rain
Cleansing droplets, trickling lightly
Not enough to launder away the burning
Storm, cold yet warm

Rinse out the light
Stay in my sight
Rain keep me sane

Sunsets And Rooftops

On a rooftop, swing still
Press against the edge
As I press the memories out of sight

It still burns when I close my eyes
Open, closed, awake, asleep, it's there
It seemed it be clearer up here

The only clarity I got is that it'll never stop
Still pressing
I feel everything

Press down
Glance down
Fall

Clarity is my prevalence
As I now lie still
I feel everything again one last time
I pour into the earth.

Gold

Slides and swing sets
Stars and sunsets
Time sets in line

From running through grass fields and chasing skies
Gone to running away from our lives

We were children
We're a wreck
Wreck our bike on street corners
Wreck our cars into glass houses

How did we go?
Go to your hiatus of street lights and parking lots
I'll go to mine if I can find it

Where did we go?
Out of your parents to your boyfriend's studio garage
Out of town, dreams of west coast bound
Meet again? When and where, my friendship goes with you

How did we go?
From rain splashes and painted flowers
To late night drives to nowhere and coke in bathrooms of crude
house parties
We'll carry our scars
From scraped knees to the scare of a pregnancy

Where did we go?
Maybe time will tell us someday

Sky dreams

Find a place for us outside your torn walls and broken promises
A place as bright as your intentions
Where you and I lie on freedom and times a miss

Times a burden we don't need
We just need our intertwining moments pure as twilight
I know your pain, I lost all mine when I met you
Side swept by your gallantry
Won over in an instant

I'd search galaxies and mountain tops
Galaxies physical and spiritual
To find a place your heart can lie easy

An emotional lullaby
As you are mine
For you, you have my forever

Warm

Hope is us
Hope is the light in your eyes as they trace the night sky
An attachment to the stars shining through our souls,
dragging them from the earth to something more pure

Something clear
Something true

Clearer than the atmospheric journey of light
Purer than the innocence of daydreams
Truer than your words than made us
Clear skies lead me to you

Light holds up dearly denouncing our inner darkness
Together is our truth that carries our high past the skies and galaxies
back to your eyes
Clearer than hope itself

Breathe in water

We walked to the pier
We walked into watercolors and Ferris wheels
Walked out of borderlines and tumbleweeds
Out of war stained houses and clogged pipe dreams

We should have run
Maybe we would have dodged the set years of disappointment
Liked how we dodged the hail storm of human concern
We were free on a wire line charged west

We shared a cigarette underneath the docks
Menthol millennials stuck in a Marlboro lifestyle

Spent our first night in a grungy car
Sheltered from the sky's infliction
You held my hand through the storm
I held your heart from the lighting
I wouldn't let it strike you twice

Stars poured through the sand
Placed my lips to your collarbone
Felt the shore crash in the same repetitions as we
Watched the sunset fade in the same stride you walked away with

Angel feathers

Sleep through week days
Weekends my awakening
Sleep endearing
Wake up to sun streaked windows

Fall asleep to vivid thoughts
Dreams velvet embrace
Lay soft and hushed

Bring me back to a lullaby of glimmering waters, painfully blue
Swim through my soul

I'm jealous of dream catchers
I can't hold them
I wake to often losing my feathers of hope

Pieces to wonder

Emotion flames ignite wildfire
Implosion automatic

My moments forever
More feelings than stars in the sky
Over ran in a crash course to the edge of myself
My head can't keep up with my heart

I dream in technicolor embers
Awake drowning in insipid charcoal
Kaleidoscope wishes crushed by glib blockades
I collect the opalescent fragments and ponder my pixie dust

Frail

Frail hairs break away, sullen wings collapse
A weakened breath dies out a heart sunken
Nailed claws bloody and worn tear and grasp
To reach a place once lost, to soar once again

Bewildered into ailment, collapse
Vanity sunken bruised over inflation
Gravitational chains cause a relapse
Fallen into limbo without hesitation

Struggling to reach pure air up above
To reach the bright hazy rays soaring once more
Redemption strived for, float free to the gates of love
Burden lifted a weary door opened

Chains now broken, fall into a worn empty ground
Spirits awaken glory again found

To stars and rain

Summer day in Falls highlight
Winters calling sanity
October's bearings
carry July envy

I can't hold time
Like summer skies can't hold rain
I'm captured in the midst

Satellite wishes pull earths captivity
Drowning nature's notion in cold sweeps

Night terrors

Star light

Star bright

Decays tonight

A whisper, a gleam haunts my dreams

Tonight, they fall

Shining

Awaken

Create a new tomorrow
Lose sight of past sorrow

Indifference and cautions haunting
Fade tomorrow
Tomorrow is anew

New is cleansing
New is reviving
New is me, new is you

Be tomorrow

Break

Say anything and everything
In my mind I'm free
In reality I hate me

Forever I can see that I can never be
Break
Break away

Like the tiny embers of my soul drifting softly into the barren landfill
Barren like my heart
Chipped away once marble now to dust

Break
Break apart
What's left till I'm nothing as I've known I would be

To be me
To be free
Be gone

I'll never call home

Travels along an empty roadside
Every path seems to lead here
City lights blare out but don't call home

Groups barricade entrance of contentment
Walked past an abandoned building
Windows smashed
Paint worn

Saw my reflection in its trance

Till morning

I'll feel it when I feel it
Not this lapse
Good nostalgia
Bitter sweet memories to where I grew up
Most call it home, I guess

I walked through the old neighborhood
Street name ostracization
Cross road toxic nostalgia

Fields turn silver, under golden sunlight
Shoes stay on telephone wires
Names fade out

I saw someone I used to know somewhere
Chipped fence
Chalk washed stained dreams
Swing set over hills

I reach the end of the block
Someday I'll feel it

Animal instinct

A wolf cry at night
Awakens my sight
To see nothing, but paw prints

Legacy

You raised us on history, not just our own
Man, of the world, you tried to teach us above
I try to carry your truth and teachings

You say nature's your god
You say live free, but think of your actions
You say the world will show you what it is

A man who always seemed more demigod
Power of a storm
Even as a child I saw nothing could hold you down, you never let it happen

You were our savior as you still held your life roles
Respected by all, running your own world

You saved us from the start
From the common tragedy of our lives forthcoming, saved us
Saved from violence
Abandonment
Predators
Crystal scattered on the floor
Resentment
Being unwanted

You our protector

You showed us more
We are more
We're the strength of your bloodline
More than the world set for us
More than our birth scars
More than angry ghetto children
More than our past tragedies

I rise from your teachings
I carry your truth
I am your legacy

Shore

Sand particles immense endless
Carrying magnetically across your skin
Sun reeling surrounding all

Washed over motionless
Body left
You're just a heartbeat

Waves crash roaring out rapidly
Blankets of icy blue cradling you to where you have always been
Home is sea

Sweeping comfort
Eternal solved
A place I belong

Horizon

Eyes are mind
Mind is sight

Deliver me from flight
Fright of your departure

Body is soul
Soul is mine

Carry me from fright
Fright of your demise

Vagabond sneakers

Death autumn lights
Nights drowns day

Clouds rain swelling wells
Swimming wishes shore shocked

Wind carries whispers
Walked past blurred cars
Gave into the city's pulse

City lights suffocate stars
We are stardust

Picture frames

Summer days
Summer rain

It could never rain enough, nor could a summer day be bright enough
Acid washed memories burn vividly from heart to fingertips
Not sharp, just real

Wistfully sparking in a place that lost its own depth
I won't diminish your hurt by saying I understand how you feel
Your pain is your own

I still see it
Behind iridescent pale blue, I can't help but stare into
When you remember
When I feel you
I feel all felt

I see it in the presence of your stories
And in moments were just quiet
I sense the emotion
I sense you

I see you as my light, and pure darkness couldn't wash it out
Your inner darkness never shocked me
Your lights brighter when you let it be
That's what I see

Sadness in summer
Summer moments burn dear

Suffocate

Red pours
Rushing out fluid from earth
To suffocate the innocent
Once more

Ruined

You were a child who lived in a broken house
Shattering on the center of a cul-de-sac
Family planted in dark secrets
Blood would pour if uncovered

Silence outlasts history
Death over took offenders, evil pair
Freed by the grave, unlike all they left feeling sickeningly ruined from
there unwanted actions

My blood still pours from your same tragedy and the mess they left
I was a child left at that house

I feel tainted in every breath
Dark memories elude
Masked by self-sedation

I can feel the eyes of the world and don't want to be seen

My conscience tries to erase to freedom of mind and self
My torment woven in the dust of my past
My mind drifts like the catacombs of Paris
Searching

Drift

Wind blows
Sky snows

Time slows
It goes

With you
With I
With All

Fall back to earth

Words escape
Stained everywhere
Tainting my eternity

Everywhere I don't want to be
I see everywhere corner to corner
I feel all
I try to cloud my thoughts
A blinding light killing my haze of peace
Blazing through me
Igniting everything
Paralyzed thought stuck on repeat
I'm stuck in nightmares posing as daydreams

Montionless fear inducing panic
I can't force myself awake
I can lie still in a dreamless trance filled by darkness
Blinding burning light
Transfixing my energy before I can even breathe
Take every breath along with my thoughts

Drive

Roads over skies
Tires tread bare

Race to open valleys and pockets of plush earth
Untouched by suburbia

Touch of dusk
Enthralled in journey

Take me to a place where we can smoke in the sun
Talk the day into night
I'll drive if you lead
Just please don't leave

As one

You took me in light
Your look made me burn heaven's grace
You were always something I wanted to know
Never thought I could have

The world disappeared when you held my hand
My world brightened by your being
I could have looked in your eyes like peering into the milky way
Forever chasing stars
Find peace in the outer limits
Pressed into a moan against your collarbone
Tangled in midnight, we sank into sunset

Breathless
Envious of time
I fade into seconds against your skin
I wish I could grasp time like how I'm grasped against your embrace
I wish I could grasp the sun like your warmth

Tongue trails nearly down to where my heart sank
You had me every minute
With minutes to forever
We sank into one

In dreams we can't trust

Holding onto me like a bad dream I'm stuck in
I can't sleep deep nightmares steal my reality
Let me sleep but I won't dream
My dreams my nightmares they all consist of blank fear

No longer my reality to hold
Trapped empty illusions
Numb my mind till it's blank

To help get through another day
Smoke all my hauntings away

Hold my peace
Shatter it to pieces

Dagger

Drain me
Puncture my life
Still frame our blurred end
Capture my delusion of daydreams
Drain me

Follow

Foot step
Foot step
Tread and drag

Heart beat
Heart beat
Skip away, race to convulsions
My heart follows your footsteps

I can't catch your rhythm
As you leave and return at a frequent inconsistent instance
But I trail along, entangled in your laces

Trace my heart with your eyes
I give you my all in plain sight

Tread lightly on my heart
And I'll tread light with my words

Wanderlust

Run
Ran
Running
Runaway
Go
Going
Go away
Gone
So far
Far away
Far as far will allow
Forevermore I will run
Away
Away from here
Away from me
Away from you
Away from them
Away from all
Away, away
Free to fly high

Embers

I wish I could flick away my feelings like cigarette ash
You burn like a cigarette

Common and quickly
Enclosing all in brutal warmth
Crisp smoke

Cool swarming clouds will carry me out
You'll burn out
At your own flame
I touched your jawline
You erased my mind

Waterfalls

We swam in the sunset
Laughter was our waves
Memories our tidal pool

I'd stay here forever become part of the stream, whisk us into
everlasting exultation

Moonlight in your eyes
Tears in a dear moment
Masked by waterfalls of our deliriant bliss

Looking out a window to nowhere

My sky is grey
Raining transparency

Emptiness flowing easily
That's the only recognition a numb sensation in my veins or lack of

Pathway to my mid
It's been bulldozed

Window to my soul
A mirror reflecting blank imagery

Physical being
Trapped physically
To emotionally blank to even leave the physical
At least to leave would be something

Snow Dreams

Numb, heartless, reckless
A product of your apathy
I sleep in ice

You lie in the remnants of my heart torn from my sleeve
Warped words
Dragged out
Force of karmic truth

Back to Summer Avenue

Walking just as aimlessly as our conversation
Leads us to corners of rain filled ledges
Guides us in loops of sky light fading off

The contrast of your hoodie pressing harshly against the faded adobe
neighborhood
I felt each glance

I knew your actions, thoughts as if I had a preview in slow motion
Maybe I just knew you
Or was deluded by ego to think so

I don't remember a word we said
I remember the elated easiness from our innocence

I remember you as a first
Barely remember
Pushing nostalgia haunts
You just held my hand
We went nowhere
Saw everything

I'm glad we didn't jump that fence you kissed me against
Evenings glow peering through chain-link
It was just a kiss on Summer Avenue where we left our twilight in
fleeting moments of reality

Past of truth
Learnt truth
Easily left alone
Never to look back the same

Dream Away

Drowning from the atmosphere, thrown into collision
Falling, downwards to nowhere
Beyond a point of sorrow

Shallow breath
Sorrowful tension

Pathetically I crawl to you, past you, past me, as you already have
Again, and again to the pain I should avoid I draw to instead
Toxic souls in constant collision

Drag out, crash out
For what
So, what
What if it's all gone?
What if I'm gone?
Gone going nowhere, just as we always have been

Burn

Wisps, cool grey twirling
From lips to the edges of my fingertips
Where I once held you
They fade rugged

Circling, drifting clouds disperse before I can grasp, scream, hold on
The vapors disperse drearily

I release more and more from the embers, inhale to my mind to my
heart my veins anything that'll hold
Please
Hold
I need it again
I can take it again
I'll drag it out
Again, and again
Forever I could

Swirling, mystifying haze hold me in your embrace forever
I'll stay in the waves of disillusion
Please
Stay

The world in a haze
smoke filled hope
caressing inner demons

Smoke to my freedom
Till my mind can be
I'll hold this hit like a spirit
To cleanse my own

Morning glory

Leaves in a gutter
Smoke in my window

Mind a haze
I barely feel where I am
I look out
See nothing but sunlight

Feel the suns warmth
Know I still exist
It's enough for now

Empty Bags, Empty Bottles

Can I go back
Back to a place before this feeling
Sinking
Slowing
Consumption of harsh reality

My pills have always tasted better
Nothing bitter in my sedation
Fleeting high
Sobriety's crash
Existential plunge

I leap, not ready
Nothing beautiful in my real view
Only an endless feeling to chase

Chasing clouds
Chasing dreams drowned in a wishing well
Chasing unknown embers in the sky
My chase all nothing but to fall off the edge
High is an instant
Never enough

Lashed

Maybe our crash course collision was hopeful infatuation
You're uptown
Social friends spent life styles
Ecstasy of boredom
I'm downtown
Outcast from births dedication
Built of daydreams and bottle cap borders

You go to bonfires in the valley
Every minute is with some friend or forced facade
I extinguish the trashcan bonfires of my mind
I can handle being alone
Drugs are your fun, my escape

You'll never care just do another line and go to some house party
I have my vices, but none have ever been people
Yeah, I will probably take my pills
Smoke till my minds obliviated
Medicinal daze hoping it heals my scars
I'll be on a rooftop or stairwell
Pen and pipe in hand
Both running true
Unlike you

Guide Me

Your words melt poetry
Vivid and endearing
They give me beyond tomorrow

You make days seem more
More aside just marks to cross out
You wrap time beyond this body

I'm renewed by sunset
Vibrant warmth of silk
So warm draping through my skin

Midnight draws me near
Encasing my bones drowned in indigo
Lead my starlight

Guide me beyond what I know
Rewrite my time to better beginnings
Reset me

I want to be new

Seasons

Fell to my knees to see the stars clearly
Under the winter fog
I look towards the horizon

I used to know, not all but enough
Times steals my visions
Winter snow drowns me
Cold air solid in my lungs, harsh cold

I can't breathe
I can't sleep
I can't feel right
I can't catch my moment

Spring melts the retention of my depression
hold me to summers rays
Bear me to the skies
Put my heart at ease
I know who I am in summer

Bounds

Couldn't feel anything

except water

I may not have been in as I closed my eyes

Still vision

Dark

Steal the last of my light

Still water

Stillness of breath

Still I feel, nothing in everything

Like this water, moving yet in one spot

Internal struggle freeing in the tides

Borders

Your words drip slow, like rum
Sweet and intense
Laced spiced invigoration
Flaming my blood flow
Bitterly hot

Pumping in my heart
Toxic flow
I can only hope for sweet relief
I want water of Lethe

My existence has always been bleak
Forget tomorrow, as I would be
remembered, easily not

My words drip like honey
Heavy sweet and dwindling
Wash out like rains transparency

Wash me away with the weather
I'll flow in the wind

Burn my passion in the sun

Sonnet I

Another broken promise gone astray
Weary eyes meet undetermined lies
Locked by bloodlines dreary and worn away

A splitting image links us as allies
Appearances although deceive abide
Picture frames strung from a concealed web
Into risen flames, take another step

Will our hidden difference subside?
Gone away said to return another day
Abandoned and unwanted left at bay
Smoke fills the air, are you even truly there?

A mirror image draws us close
But your fake persona divides us most

Whiskey Dreams

Soft light a glow hazy sweet
Pillow talk
Haunts my thoughts

Requiem composed for sight
It is sought
Caught up deeply

My own night terror awakening
Whiskey draw me to sleep
Dark guides to darkness
Sleep deprived envy
Flowing heavy like liquor

Shots in the dark
Taken in sequence to sleep
Moonlight ending dawn arising
plunging my dreams to a lull of you

Leaving my nightmare quite true

I

I can't even keep smoke a float
Grey clouds crashing down
Sinking boat
Anchor around my throat

Carry my words down
With the weight you left me

Ashes burn from my fingertips
Trailing down like false glitter wishes
My room is filled with smoke dreams
That fade like I
I am transparent, never enough
Just fading in all lives I touch

You left nothing
As I was left to feel like
I never knew nothing, could contain so much

Once Upon

Sunlight on my skin, cool earth beneath
Dug my fingernails into the balance
Trying to hold the feeling

A place I exist for sole existence
Freedom of heart
Where I am gold, not broken
As the world once was and may lay underneath

Lost in a daze
Mind a haze
Days going on forever

Haze for days
Trapped laze
Find ways in sun's rays

Soft earth clay
Encasing sink in
Soft craze

I can be here awhile
Seeping blended visions
To find my golden core

Kiss Past Midnight

Winter's grace
Coveted under star filled skies
Felt a light from you in every touch

Numb to the cold
Guided to warmth by your lips
You're being to mine, us giving all

You kissed me
And you kissed me
You kissed me deep
And I became

Forever dreaming

Search for me in moonlight
I'll chase away day to hold this feeling
Warm embrace in every touch
I trace every line of you
You my North star

I watch you in moonlight
Serene lucidity
I feel dizzy and elated locked in your trance
You have tunnel vision to my heart with just your glance

I never want to lose this image
Us in moonlight
You my guiding light

Ease

Drunk off summer skies
I feel a warmth wash over me
I can't feel time

I want to see something beautiful
I want to feel as such
My tongue is numb like my mind

Draw near

Heaven sent curse
Set upon an engraved birthstone
Smoke clouds haze the skies symbols

Fogged imagery
Pouring cloud tunnels
Inducing toxicity
Standing on a ground set to crumble

Namesake, forsaken
Not given
Fading a fate line crossed
Leaving a bullet of conscience
To erase the last